Home is a Place Worth Burying

Poems by
Haley Thompson

IØ163422

Up On Big Rock Poetry Series

SHIPWRECKT BOOKS PUBLISHING COMPANY

Raising independent publishing to the level of indie music & film

PO Box 20
Lanesboro, MN 55949

IN®
DIE

Cover design by Shipwreckt Books
Cover photo *Fallen Leaves* by Kendra Shirey

© 2013 Shipwreckt Books
All rights reserved
ISBN-10: 0989586111
ISBN-13: 978-0-9895861-1-5

First Printing

Acknowledgments

I am grateful to the editors of *Forge Journal* for first publishing "Honesty".

Thank you to my friends and family who helped to encourage an inspire me while writing these poems, including Kendra Shirey for her amazing photographs.

Huge thank you to Tom Driscoll for taking a chance, and walking me through this first publication.

Table of Contents

When you open your mouth,
those beautiful lips,
to yawn in the Midwest, winter plains

the sound like a seashell to an ear
and burdening howl.

Above the wind, the night is bleakest.
And supple. Close the lips
around that daft wind
and blink.

Poetry

In this there is skin
of men and trees.
The season of lime, and sugar
in the glass.

In this there are trees.
The way the sun hits,
all of us in this,
it was once warm.

And this is cut from
the center of the field.

Where the pearl may grow,
or bury, and from the center
you will feel birds.

I am talking about cards and seed.
I am talking about the dust of this house.

Or I am not talking about poetry
and I am listening to the light through the stalk.

Happiness

When I saw it, I knew how not to touch it.
I knew how to abandon it at the base.

Its surface was pearly, but still. If it had been
yesterday or maybe, 2008 I could've managed

to pick it up, gauge it, maybe even pocket it
for the summer or a quick drink. But now, you see

it's not so easy. It has grown heavy. It has grown
roots. I too have grown. As if that summer, sitting

in the parking lot playing Tecate to The Kinks –
I have become more cement. Have wanted

dogs too, to follow me up a trail. For someone
to take my picture in the reflection of a subway

passing a mural, painted as a map of a body,
on fire, facing forward, moving on.

Common Alder

And this is a fenceless thing,
the forest, a body,
amazing when it stands.

Overhead,
I'd just seen a white oak
full of mistletoe.

There, a piece of jade fell,
I mean cedar,
and I took it to be your eyes.

God, you are beautiful.

Fanned trees
strewn, or burnt open.

This was a mild timber.
This was your voice a well chime.
Your outline, milk light, a stratum.

The Square in Spring

1.
Like the weak
or the bee that flew into me
on the first hot day,
hitting twice the nape of my neck.

This unnoticed as of the wind,
and the things spinning in the square:

leaves, paper like leaves, nests, cotton threads.

The square only in wood benches;
and when you read, people vanish.
And when you turn people replenish.

The portrait holding the man;
Artist hands are approaching.

We agreed in reasonable.
His hands are moving in shapes
my person cannot help.
The sun turned my face to petal hues.

The artist leaves; my face in his hands.
I situate and sit back into the square.

Women with their figures and fingers on their hips.
Children, eyes sewn with wind.

Me, I might ash into my shoe.
Thinking, if my toes touch those embers,
my feet may turn to flowers.
It is spring.

Mud plumes from the river's earth.
Water the weeds with wine we bring
to the river; springs offering:

2.
Ducks and their lungs,
like ours, similar,
on water.

Vivid spectacle the lights upset of the water.

My feet may turn to flowers
at the mouth of summer's river.

Pairs in feet become in spring.
Wind distracts in couples:

Feathers, eyes, waves and cusps of waves.

Currents wash cherries for the birds,
the river becomes swallows.
The birds become night.

The sky is breaking; lilaceous.
Night disperses into black birds,
Feathers on their wings.

Wind gathers me in distracted parts of spring.
Petals of my skin loosen.
My feet bloom into flowers and fauna.
I break when sky breaks.
Disperse into river, the spring, the square.

Gone

You wanna go
as far into the woods as they will have you.
I hear you. And I'll raise you.

Take you two steps further into the frozen river.
In the midst of July. With my feet on fire.

You wanna invite me in
and make me dinner. Do home-like things.

I will teach you the origin of taste.
Sleep in your bed and take a bath.

Leave an earring in a drawer,
write my height on your wall.

You have to tell me all of my flaws
or else they don't exist.

You have to tell me when to go
or I won't begin to pack.

And if I forget something
I never want to come back.

This is the way to my heart,
straight through the wall,
on the other side, sky.

Line Between Friendships

Two grey horses, flea bitten grey,
as it was told to you —
you studying them,
before you knew them,
on the hillside, where they fed.

At night among them we would lay, tilted
upwards, practicing the speech of this place,
Toponas, yarrow root. Hush.

Remember the girl, falling off Apache.
She looked flat against the moonlight
like paper. Something needing
to knock the wind.

It gets to the point where
you lose grips you never had,
probably anyway. Thinking thoughts
of how human these animals can be.

Let them nibble off your shoulder
like a lover. Tell them things
about the divorce, your lost faith,

your sister's hardships.

Rely on them to take you
only so deep into the river.

Rise up, so you may sleep
in the company of herds.

Where The Sky Ends Or Begins

Had you known the thing planted
was meant for you,
you may never have gone down that road.

Where it took you, you chopped wood at the beach
for what seemed like the best years.

When you turned around and led it back home,
you couldn't love a woman anymore,

the way a horse could understand you.
So, you picked up where you had never started.

You must touch the back of the ankle lightly.
It's like talking but not saying words.

Or maybe it's like saying what you should have,
the last time you touched her.

The way the dog loves the trimmings
of a horse's hoof
is how I remember you younger. A slow
hammering

and the way your shadow looked,
holding the horseshoe to the sky for good luck.

Placing Bets

It was flooding, the summer
I destroyed myself in equal halves.
One for wanting and one for having.

You remain the center and the edge
of my first damaged self, the good half.
Rocking gently between dust and water.

As it goes, anyway, you survived.
I left traces of myself, knowing I would leave.
Touching light fixtures, a note in the glove box.

You were mapped in my poems, successfully.
I thought of you when it rained, when I made eggs.
The smell of wood smoke and sand.

These things we mean to ruin
come back in more pieces.
It is complicated the way time works. Stubborn,

breathing the tide, furthering
the branch from the tree.

It will one day be gone, the halves melding.

Approaching state lines and old lover's bodies.
Sometimes I think I know your curve
better than my own.

It is all leading up to the places we are now broken.
I can't see a man's watch without
touching my own wrist to my cheek.

Suffices to say, that which we stole
we could never keep.
I lost prints of myself to the sun,

the pavement, cotton.
Every bit trying to collect itself within your home.
In equal halves: when I am not there I am there,

am never there again.

Morning With Maps

Where are we?
A grass field?
Shutter-grass or wheat?

It doesn't matter,
there is no shadow
only silo.

Walk from the porch
out toward the wood pile.
Over the stream.

It looks like cedar,
shaped as the backbone of a girl.
Don't walk down it, walk over it.

This is a map
of where things don't end, but sky
is reflected on the land.

Across the water
you see a woman out there, barely.

She's washing her hair, under the faucet,
next to a garden.
Her hair, like the hands of a river.

Follow the gravel
toward the gate,
then past the bend.

End up in turnips and beet.
Wash in maps
of houses near gardens.

Housekeeping

In palpable mornings
the dew will gather under
the length of your fingernails.

Skin so taunt and turned from me,
you slip like pearls.
Even the hue you are,
now dusty or mineraled or stolen.

In evenings when it seems spiting,
my heels that grope this ground slip.
Saved by your hands lifting my hair.

Had we stayed in these woods,
the roof would have fallen.
Your tendence to stand in it.

The lake gathered aged to your toes
and those as pearls I felt curl.
My lips chipped and stuck to the polish you wore.

You said, had I eyes to see the ocean in your pores,
disrupt would taste different to me.

I could was the ocean in my cheeks,
glimpse seeds in your eyes.

Honesty

Be that when you hold in your mouth
the bones that roll against your teeth
you are being honest in your destruction.

Hold truth self evident, in each scar you touch
on another, in places only you have allowed
yourself to go. Because this is your day

and those who pay for it alone in bare rooms,
on floors making and unmaking a mound
of themselves that will never set. A vocabulary

from the drips of a horse's mouth, she said
and I let her. Us who walk with our passion shied
need not a finger toward the sky. To know the wind

is blowing is to feel it and it is right.
Tonight dream big. Sleep out in the field
among the herd. In the daylight

bring it inside with you.
We are burning our way through this,
root and all.

A Difficult Biology

For Ari Bar-Mashiah

Have you heard the one about the vertebrae?
I could hardly believe it myself.
But I've been digging

and turns out we did all once have tails.
That's when I thought of you, and then I didn't.

Humans had voices then,
voices that said something
in a language of questions.
Since then, we have found ourselves

stuck in beds that speak a new language.
Forcing us to think of some kinder words to say.

It's funny, when you walked me
from the synagogue
to the flood museum,
I thought I saw you lingering slightly,

between orchestra and the Attempts at Relief,
turning in curtsy, trying to hear the joke in midair.

Passing Through

Roots of the ironwood fed ghosts here,
to rise and howl.
Years before, just visiting, I had touched
dust on the mantel
of a house with no children.

I wrote a letter here once
to get to the Carolinas.
I still remember which one.
 It landed in Alabama.
 I'm sure it was burnt before it was read.

I return again to teach myself
and there are pockets in this dream,
pockets or cracks.

This place, god love it,
sweaty and angry
has written itself by tradition of men
lost and wondering.
Lost, but oh, so brave.

Wondering and deaf.

Heads turn from here
and keep moving.
Jumping,
we are calling it, *Mississippi*.

Home Is A Place Worth Burying

a potted plant of ivy or aloe.
We'd watched the storm come in
from Cedar and Boone,
folding itself out
a map across your lap.

Spreading in fingers, in ants,
black birds woke the sky with
sounds of insect wing and caw.

Earlier that day, in morning
you said the pasture
was the color you thought a shell could be,
pressing your ear
towards where the storm was carrying,

sounds to mute the birds,
quiet the ocean from the shell.

What Might Have Happened, If It Had

All morning sitting here, facing
the walnut tree, the arbor you made

winding one tree into another.
The arbor, it bends over the summer squash.

Remember how the seeds felt. Your hands
pulling weeds. All morning sitting facing out

sketching your feet on the porch-rail and the brush
fields behind them. The house beyond that

has no one to paint it. The chimney still smokes,
occasionally. The house you sit outside of

there's no one to answer the way the wind hits it.
The tear in the screen has curled and opened, into

the shape of a flower someone once brought you.
A black-eyed Susan? Peace lily for your wedding.

Off toward the walnut tree the bark is open,
where you thought he was living, once in a dream.

Land and Sky

Leaf caught under thin ice
a water frame.

I poked at it with
a feather from my pocket,
                                    or wing.

It, the leaf, was red.

What heard of bitter wing samples.
Am I so grateful enough or welcomed
to move pasture to hollow?

Spiced cattail to linnet.
Hill over hill, over steep flourish.
Land repeats itself in lilac, in thistle.
Churns itself, a furrow.

Watch your step when the land,
covered in snow, won't part from the sky.
It is important, the ground, unmoving.

If you look, look closely.

The leaf was a fish we meant to catch,
when the water was still running.
Carrying itself, a wing.

Liven Against This Rock, Unmelting

This is a geode.
I gave it to you from Belle Plain.
That time when we drove on through,
and no one noticed.

Where we'd stopped
you pulled the picture
from the book.

The willow he'd planted, the shed,
a map cut-out where home was.

Forgot the grey a mountain could be.
The fields and sky in Storm Lake,
when your hands are cold, but your body is hot.

When you wish for a porch,
or money, but we keep driving.
Windshield our porch,
our bay window.

I count each town name
on fence posts:

Adair, Globe, Blythe.
Some bone-garden,
some dust-hive.

At a pull off, near Look Out Point,
You handed me a dogbane.
We'd driven years.

We are handing things back and forth.
Each town a knur,
silence to rend us on home.

Light Bug

We wanted to measure
                        the weight of the sky.

As children we will, we built ourselves
                a foot-bridge over the stream.
You caught minnows and let the go,
                            watching them,
their tails, bodies of dancers.

I caught light bugs in jars,
undid the lid under the water.

You said, *it's not the same*,
but I knew for sure
            one was a fish inside
and you were wrong.

Years later, driving, we are not children,
a light bug could hit your window,
you would reach out and get it for me,
or write *Hello* with it   and your finger,

we are not children.

That time you trail your fingers up my arm,
sometimes against my will,
        you take a light bug and crush it to my arm,
trail the light up the inside, toward my elbow.

Hands lace my ribs, slight biting,
measuring the weight of you.

When we are driving,
we are not the children we were,
moving across these fields,
measure the sky from the ground.

Pomona

1.
Smooth is this clandestine garden,
or your hands
actions of the gardens primula;
the garden sound,
wet bloom thicken the soils stomach
collecting squash pear, and hoary morning apple.
Generous rounded forms
of seedpods and gourds.
Something pressed us
in separate music,
the light ice made.

Soaps of trailing bind weed,
lathers of heartsease is our ocean.
We delight himself in whales of lime grass.

"When your bones are shapes of boats,
you are one water recites..."

Water gathers ice while walking;
water gathers holiday.

"Savored calling birds on stopping tides.
You will notice the twelfth of stopping in the birds.
The severity is calling when stopped…

                              lovely."

We walk this span of iced light.
Be careful not to loosen the falls
of bird-peaches.
Pearls the peaches we drown, these birds seem birds
we indulge. Purge of tree dropping birds we release;
our arms are bark for now, our bones are boats
thank loud.

2.
"Their hands are not mist, or bark, or fruit we
have…"
Something blue in eyes we shrink,
there is no   stepping

me,

        we needed to leave.

It is morning and I had two.
My eyes water away this wind
in tunnels.
Nothing most of what is right,

the letters made of birds I see.

My wait is worth of wind.

Birds in twelve of them I bake with calling hands.
Fruit and all, we venture home away.

People sinking; their skin lacks bark.
Their bones lack boats.

Our water does the calling from the bridge.

And the garden we returned, away from this and
holidays. These days are less to be of opened end as
to be of humid winters. The January I enclose
without the talent of. The garden encapsulates,
exists inside the milky steams of dandelions, the
whiskers of these spidery legs handwriting is, I hang
toward the growing of these leaves under ice.

You shed

my reflection off the bridge,

our boats come out of us.
Sinking are the prints of plights.

Snow-petal

It's me,

I dreamed we were trees facing each other.
Our hands were the same hands
and it snowed corners.

But the snow was light
and the corners of each snow-petal

were letters someone wrote
in a vegetable garden.

Two pieces of snow were a recipe,
most were an apple seed.

The way you looked,
branches from your body.

We just faced each other,
but were as trees
and did not blink.

Send More Flowers

For Amanda Nadleberg

Write yourself a spring with buds and berries.
You are a writer, the sky can be all wisteria,
or pilot glass, if you want it too.
Eat a lattice heart, from the shell, and drink wine.
Write yourself a hat while you're at it.
It doesn't have to be fancy.
It's not like you are a bee keeper,
unless you want to be.
Write a new face in the mirror,
a face the boy on the bus would have married,
because you thought he would ask.
Now, because I reminded you,
write a glass in your hand, and drink up.
Don't be found out.
Don't forget your hat.

Poet Farmer
For Tom Driscoll

Searching the long headed trees,
north towards Sugar Bottom,
once, where a poet could live.
There within moss was fire.

He a moon or a man,
became, inside the groans.
A certain begonia took him, husbanded.

Fox glove and sesame, a morning glory farmer.
Once never within the world
without a dog or basil at hand.

And blue was the color day.

Have myself brave rooted in witch hazel,
my kind, moon-hearted, poet farmer.

How to Build

This morning, when you woke
you had slept outside,
but couldn't remember
how you got there.

Dew had caught a spider web
between you and who you thought
was someone you once knew,
but was instead barely a thistle growing.

It's hardening when these things happen,
The house won't listen, or notice
but it cowers as you cower. The lattice work
you think you carved, or someone did

you used to know, is starting to break free.
Are the notes in the ring box your writing
or someone who used to carve a lattice work?

Once I'd slept outside there too. Thought I saw him
just behind the walnut tree carving something
that looked like the name of a bird or a woman.

He had the long body of a fawn, sinew and limping. When I woke he was gone again, if he'd ever been.

My personal poetic Lexicon

I.

There are only two trees:

maple or apple;
also a sparrow, or root bird.

II.

To refer to a pear:

see a girl in the window, cradling a pear,
the stem against her wrist.

Think it is a sparrow no one else has noticed,
and she is eating the wing.

She is a grave.

III.

There are sometimes fruit:

lemon, orchard, pear skin;
Lemons borne of the sea.
Orchard is for where a seed belongs,
but there is wood instead.

& pear skin makes good letters.

For Citrus see also:

how to extract the seed,
without breaking the skin.

IV.

To refer to skin:

bird, milk, or rind.
Sometimes elbow, hip, or wrist;
bodies always a girl,
unless it is a spine or ankle,
 then it is a man or a willow.

V.

Always birds:

wing is attached to me in water, snow, or ice.
Often spring, few rain, unless summer.
Always petal.

If the wing is not a body it is a pecan.
Oh, and bird is also a feather, or leaf.

If ocean, than everything.
Unless pasture, then shell.

VI.

When there is a moon, there is a reflection.
A reflection is always a puddle or snow,
but never both.

As if we'd say, *scored moon bones fell*,
and that is a very good line. Ditsy moons.

VII.

There are houses:

plants, always aloe, or corn.
Bread, and milk,
means there is love, I think
Iowa is the same as corn, and soil.
See also, house.

The sun hits the silo, always.

About the Author

Haley grew up on a farm outside Iowa City, Iowa. She received her B.A in English Literature from the University of Iowa and an M.F.A. in Poetry from the Iowa Writers' Workshop. Haley was awarded a Teaching-Writing Fellow while at Iowa. Her poems have appeared in *Forge Journal*. She now lives in Nashville, Tennessee. This is her first book of poetry.

Up On Big Rock Poetry Series

is about out of silence an emergent cacophony, of
image, of imagination & is about the poets who
carry sounds one at a time like precious sparks to
the hearth : words cupped in their blistering hands,
their impatient breaths keeping alive light & heat &
racket.

& the sky turns dark greenish
if it were a bottle filled

with purpled wine & instead of
horizon there is this space

crammed if it is your mind
with your thoughts if they are

the stars

July 2013

IN®
DIE

www.ingramcontent.com/pod-product-compliance
Lightning Source LLC
Chambersburg PA
CBHW070109070426
42448CB00038B/2400